John F. Perry
Man Of The Land

By Stephen J Anderson

Copyright © 2023 Stephen J Anderson

All rights reserved.

ISBN: 9798854556880

Preface

When approached about the potential of writing this biography, it seems even the idea itself was hereditary. Sue registered her father's reflections on his past and how John remarked increasingly often that he should've written a book with all the stories he has throughout his life. Sue then suggested the idea to me about writing my own grandfather's biography around March of 2022.

My first foray into non-fiction and an entire lifetime to try and do justice. It was something of a daunting prospect. In retrospect, regardless of the final quality, I'm glad I made the attempt as learning so much about John's life was fulfilling, interesting and very often amusing.

Sue, her dog Alfy and I would visit John at his Parsonage Downs cottage as he recounted the many memories of his life whilst I recorded the audio and later transcribed these talks into written form. I've tried throughout the book to capture John's natural voice, quoting him verbatim where possible to help give you a sense of the man's character.

Succinctly, if you picture a chuckling fellow in an armchair with a toothy smile and a glint in his eye, you'll have a good idea visually of John Perry. I hope the stories that follow give you a good sense of his personality too.

I'd like to thank John's daughter and my mother Sue Anderson for her consistent and invaluable help in the discussions with John, as well as fact-checking and helping promote the book.

Thanks also to Diane Searl and Yvonne Perry for unearthing old photos or sitting down with me to hunt back through their memories. Thanks to Em Fanchette, whose assistance in proofreading makes all my books seem far more grammatically sound than in their natural state.

And of course, thank you Grandad John, for unravelling your long and storied life with your inherent wit, charm and knack for an engaging and humorous anecdote. Sadly, some of the bluer stories will have to remain unpublished in my notes but they all helped paint the picture of who you are. I feel lucky and honoured that I got to immortalise some of that person in this book. I hope you enjoy the tales herein and the portrait of the man behind them.

Stephen J Anderson. 14th May 2023.

John F. Perry
Man Of The Land

By Stephen J Anderson

A long life is not necessarily a life well-lived but in the case of John Frederick Perry, both can be confidently deemed true. A salt of the earth man who wouldn't dream of salting the earth, John's humble lifestyle belies a deep-rooted richness of character that warmed the souls of many during his many years.

Born on the 14th November in the year 1930. The first child of Alfred and Ethel Perry (Often known as "Minnie"), a farmworker and nursemaid respectively. John spent the first three years of his life at a house in Park Road, Little Easton in the greater Dunmow area of Essex. He and his parents then moved to Raven's Cottage next to the consistently named Raven's Farm, where Alfred worked a large part of his life for a man named Humphrey Trembath.

This would mark the second of only three different homes John would live in throughout his life. While he enjoyed many holidays and trips with family, John was decidedly a local man through and through. He was content and settled in his surroundings which became only more evident through his commitment to local events and enriching the village of Little Easton and the lives of those within it.

Little Easton, as the name implies, is a small village and civil parish dating back to the 12th century. In 2011 its population was a little over four hundred making it a tight-knit, friendly community. Its natural countryside beauty attracts extensive farming and hobbyist fishermen. It's this farming lifestyle that John would inherit and prove his talent for.

"I'd just fallen off a table."

At the age of five, John began education at Little Easton school. The same small establishment his father attended back in 1912. The first of his brothers, Geoffrey, born in March 1933, would later join him at this school although John recalls his brother's absence many times, due to Geoffrey's lifelong struggles with asthma and respiratory illness.

Alfred and Ethel's third son and John's second brother Peter, was born in July 1938 and finally, a daughter Judy in April 1946. The late 1930's had John and Geoffrey both attending school and by 1939, John talks of his first memories of the second World War. These included the children bringing compulsory gas masks into school with them and classes often being interrupted with swift detours into nearby air raid shelters.

A school photo from 1936. John is the third from the left on the front row.

At home as well, air raid sirens were a common cacophony growing up and the Perrys actually dug their own shelter at the bottom of the garden. A deep trench surrounded by galvanised steel sheeting. Oftentimes around two in the morning, the siren would start blaring and the family would have to rush down to the shelter trench in their pyjamas.

Eventually Ethel Perry grew weary of this cold and muddy midnight sprint and decided they'd all had enough. Despite the risk, from then on they stayed in the house as the air raid sirens wailed around them.

During the blackouts, John and his family would shut out all light with black roll-down blinds on the windows. With no electricity at the time, they managed equipped with only dim paraffin lamps for seeing. The Home Guard, an armed citizen's militia during the second world war, would routinely patrol during these blackouts and bang on the doors of any homes still displaying any light from inside.

Despite growing up in such uncertain and perilous times, John and Geoffrey developed a mutually mischievous nature and John recalls this often landing on their long-suffering father. "Yeah, we used to play him up, me and Geoffrey. With him being deaf you know." While not profoundly deaf, Alfred's hearing did deteriorate significantly over time but all this meant for John and Geoffrey's childish pranks was an amusing exploitable blind spot, so to speak.

John recounts one time, where Alfred's temper was pushed to its limit. "He went into a little passageway where the playroom was. He'd got several walking sticks there and he got one of his sticks out. 'I've had enough of you little buggers' he said. Swung up with the walking stick, hit the ceiling and down comes the ceiling. Me and Geoffrey were out the door and we waited 'til mother come home. Let him explain it to her" and no doubt face the aftermath.

A quirky aside to this story came about from my own confusion of Alfred being fairly young at this point but still using a walking stick. These days more commonly seen as a necessity and medical aid, a walking stick back in those times could as easily have been just an accessory.

For those living in fairly rural areas as the Perry family did, it could also serve as a useful path-clearing nettle whacker...or less useful ceiling whacker in Alfred's case. He owned four or five walking sticks but saw no need for glamour or extravagance and kept them in a detached piece of drainpipe in the passageway. This is indicative of a make-do and mend attitude that John himself certainly inherited.

The ripples of the war emerged again as John and Geoffrey returned home from school one day. Their mother had vaguely warned them there would now be strange people about in wartime. A group of black American soldiers happened to be nearby and John recalls the then frightening question posed to them. "Would you like some candy, kids?"

As two young boys from a rural part of South East England in the 1930's they not only had no knowledge of American accents or the slang for sweets but had never seen a black person in their lives before either.

John and Geoffrey fled home to their mother who later retold the tale to their father.

"The boys have got frightened, seen some black men."

"They're harmless enough" their father explained. "They're good old boys. They're laying cables to Easton Lodge Park where all the trees are being felled. They're gonna lay concrete runways, turn it into an airfield."

This nearby airfield would soon become a familiar part of the scenery for John growing up. He recalls the twin engine Marauder Bombers that were housed there once the construction was completed. "When we heard them revving up to go out on a raid, we used to run to the perimeter track.

"That's meself, Geoffrey and brother Peter by this time, and watch them take off. Four or five hours later we could hear the roar as they were coming back home so we rushed to the perimeter track again to watch them land. Some with only one engine, full of bullet holes and some with their undercarriage shot away."

With the Americans at least, there was scarce enough security that soldiers wouldn't repel onlookers and would even invite children onto the aerodrome to look around sometimes. The planes and runways became regular sights and play areas for John and his brothers.

Around this time there are also unconfirmed rumours involving stolen flares and fireworks or even getting inside one of the gliders and bailing shortly before take-off. Never straying into delinquent behaviour or vandalism "The Perry Boys" would come to be known for their light-hearted mischief around the village.

John remembers seemingly endless evacuees moving to Little Easton and the surrounding areas, where eventually some became permanent residents. Though while many children living in urban areas experienced relocation during the war, John and his brothers were distanced and rural enough that their trips away from home were only necessitated briefly.

The practice of billeting is broadly that of providing temporary accommodation for people. Sometimes in a military context but for young John and Geoffrey it involved staying with relatives or family friends while a newborn sibling required more focused immediate care.

With the birth of their younger brother Peter in 1938, John and Geoffrey stayed with three different households for a fortnight each. The first two weeks were with "Uncle Jim and Auntie Winnie." living at the Park Road house where John was born. This was followed by Mrs Thorogood, a family friend living in Mill End and then finally the Halls family.

Billy Halls was a foreman at Buildings Farm in Dunmow owned by members of the same Trembath family Alfred worked for. We don't know how disruptive the Perry brothers found this period of relocation at the time but John recalls that "Dad used to come and visit us at weekends."

At eleven years old John transferred from Little Easton primary school to the only secondary school in Dunmow at that time. The three mile bicycle ride every day was a no doubt exhausting routine but one that kept John a healthy and athletic child. During this time the dangers of the war were still very present in John's life.

The Perry family avoided the worst of the conflict but there were several near misses throughout those years. John recalls plane crashes in the nearby fields and at the aerodrome, alongside bombs decimating local football pitches. One Sunday at about midday, a plane crashed just down the road from their home. John's father Alfred ran to help pull the pilot from the wreckage but his wounds from the fire had proven fatal.

Another frightening instance came indirectly from an accident up at the aerodrome. John retells how they stored bombs there and one day some kind of mistake or mishandling triggered an almighty explosion. John was at school at the time but returned home to be informed by his mother that their house had been hit by the resulting shrapnel. John collected some of this ample debris and reckons he may still have some in the shed somewhere.

Such a fraught and disrupted childhood luckily didn't hold back John's educational achievements. He excelled in most classes and after proving top of the class at thirteen, he was offered a place at a technical school in Chelmsford.

Due to the expense and logistical problems of travel, he couldn't follow up this offer and instead left school at fourteen to work with his father at Raven's Farm. The methods of this work would seem backbreaking to us now but in 1944 this form of agriculture is all there was and John's interest in all things agricultural had been budding from even younger than he was then. Suffice to say, his eventual record of work would prove it was not a decision he regretted.

Raven's Cottage in June 2022

Raven's Farm in June 2022. As a young man, John would climb the barns on the left and tar the roofs to prevent leaking.

Roughly ten employees worked at the farm growing wheat, barley, oats, sugar beet, potatoes, tares, trefoil and a variety of other crops. Tares being a type of mimic weed similar in appearance to wheat and more commonly known as darnel these days. While toxic in high quantities, it can be used for measured anaesthetic or even in beer brewing for a more dizzying kick. Trefoil, on the other hand is a low-creeping yellow perennial plant with less toxic medicinal properties and is used in sedatives, anti-inflammatory and anti-spasmodic medications.

The farm work also more directly influenced the ongoing war efforts with the type of crops produced. John explains how "during the war we went into flax and linseed. We grew acres and acres of that. There were parts of the stem I think of the flax that used to go into making aircraft or parts of aircraft."

Specifically it was fibres from the flax plant that were used to produce linen which was stretched and chemically treated to cover the wings and frames of fighter planes. These enhancements were known as "Flax fibre reinforced composites" This was intended to protect otherwise exposed parts of the aircraft from the elements, to flatten or cover certain parts for less drag and greater aerodynamics or to simply strengthen the structure overall.

Linen was in monumentally high demand during the war and flax acreage increased fourfold in many places. Flax was also used in lace, twine, rope and certain paper but the demand has never reached those heights since the war. John remarks however that you'll still occasionally see fields of linseed with its distinctive pale blue flowers due to the use of linseed oil.

John goes on to explain how "all the work was done by horses in those days because we had no tractors. One of my jobs was if a horse lost its shoes during working, I had to take it across the fields to the blacksmith in Dunmow to be shod."

John recalls this blacksmith being near to a fruit shop called "Staceys," as well as a World War One memorial constructed in 1921. The memorial is still there today, amended with names from World War Two and a listed building on the National Heritage List since 2016.

Much of Dunmow town remains unchanged since those years. The names and brands in shops come and go but the general layout and shape of the small market town remains quite similar to that which John frequented back in the forties.

John recounts one particular trip to the Dunmow blacksmith where he found himself at the back of a queue comprised of seven or eight other horses. The busy blacksmith told him to "tie the horse up to the fence, boy and go down the town if you like. It's gonna be a couple or three hours." Upon his return to the farm later that afternoon John received a stern interrogation.

"Where've you been all day boy?" Humphrey Trembath asked him.

"Well there were seven or eight horses in front of me. I had to wait me turn."

"In future, you go earlier." came Humphrey's reprimand, leaving John a little aggrieved as all the other farmhands had done the same and queue-jumping is probably quite difficult in a line of horses.

John confesses that he wasn't always so obedient at work and he alongside the other workers did employ some unorthodox farming methods in the earliest days. For horses pulling the ploughs or transporting crops and equipment by cart, they would sometimes induce greater speed by lifting the horse's tail and holding a stinging nettle to its rear. Unsurprisingly this worked but shockingly, no one took any retaliatory kicks from any of these bum-stung horses.

The farmhands were strictly forbidden from riding the horses but on one occasion, leading a horse back to farm across the fields, John decided to attempt it. With no harness or stirrups, John had to find elevation to even get atop the horse. "I got on a tree stump or summin' and then I climbed up the tree and then onto the horse."

Things seemed to be going okay until John and the horse reached a tricky slope. The horse slipped on the decline and fell with John underneath it. It's unclear if Humphrey ever learned of this escapade but it seems John was lucky enough to not be greatly nor incriminatingly injured. A wounded pride is less noticeable than broken bones thankfully. Nevertheless "I never tried that again." John concludes decisively.

The other animals tended to on the farm included cattle, sheep and pigs which were gradually fattened up to be sold at the local market on a

Tuesday. John and some of the other farmhands would drive half a dozen bullocks several miles across the fields from the farm, all the way into Dunmow town and down the main street to the market. A feat that wouldn't be possible today due to the traffic but John explains how there were almost no cars or vehicles of any kind in the area in those days and people were mainly walking or using horse and cart transport.

John and the others would trudge all the way back to Raven's Farm whilst Humphrey Trembath would go into town around two in the afternoon to see the bullocks being sold to local butchers. "If the butchers thought some of the cattle weren't fat enough Humphrey would come home and send us all the way across the fields to Dunmow again to bring the cattle that weren't sold back to the farm."

Trips of this nature didn't always run smoothly either as John remembers "On one occasion, coming in along the high street in Dunmow. We're taking two bullocks back to the farm. A shop doorway was open and the bullock tried to get in, scaring the life of the people inside."

By this time in WWII the Americans had moved out of the nearby Easton Lodge aerodrome and the RAF had moved in alongside the Women's Auxiliary Air Force (WAAF). The new aircraft John would often see there included Stirling Bombers and gliders.

The bombers, once at the forefront of aerial combat and bombardment in the war, by 1944 were relegated to troop transport in favour of the more advanced Halifax and Lancaster bombers. These Stirling bombers would instead tow the gliders full of soldiers into Germany and other conflicting countries during the Allied invasion of Europe in the final years of the war.

John recalls the vast amounts of Nissen huts which housed the soldiers. Semi-cylindrical corrugated iron structures used extensively as barracks during both the first and second world war. Another newly routine sight became the airmen and the WAAFs cycling down from the aerodrome along the footpath by Raven's Cottage. The groups would head into Dunmow town for an evening out and would return to the barracks later that night.

One evening, John remembers, one particular WAAF got a puncture and asked the Perry family if she could leave her bicycle at Raven's Cottage while she walked into Dunmow instead. They agreed and while she was gone Alfred mended the puncture for her.

The Perry family learned the WAAF's name was Ivy Wilson. Dark haired, roughly in her mid-twenties and "very pleasant" John recalls. "I wouldn't say she was attractive and I wouldn't say she was ugly. Somewhere in between."

"She got quite friendly with mother. Used to call in for tea. As Christmas approached, mother said to Ivy 'Are you going home for Christmas?'

Ivy replied 'No, my home's up north and I've only got forty eight hours leave. So by the time I got home, it'd be time to come back.'

Mother said 'you can come to us if you like.' but Ivy explained that she had prior plans to get food and drink in and have a party with the three other girls in her Nissen hut.

'Well you're welcome to come' Ethel offered regardless.

Ivy conceded but added 'I won't bring the other girls.'

So Ivy walked down to us on Christmas day," John retells, "spent the day with us. Later in the evening Ivy said 'I must be back at the base by midnight otherwise I'm in trouble.' This return journey would prove more difficult than intended however as the weather reserved no jollity for the season. "There was a gale blowing outside and it was heavily pouring down with rain. Father said to me 'You're fourteen now boy, you can see Ivy back to the base. Borrow mum's umbrella.'

So off I went with Ivy, under the umbrella. We get to the main gate and the guard shouts 'Halt! Who goes there?'

'I'm the WAAF, number...(certain identifying numbers)...Ivy Wilson'

'Who's that with you?' demands the guard.

'This young man. I've spent Christmas day with his parents and he's seeing me back.'

'Well we're not supposed to let anybody else onto the airfield' said the guard. 'But as it's Christmas day, we'll let you off.'

"So off I went with Ivy whose Nissen hut was on the far side of the airfield. We got to the hut and Ivy tapped on the door." One of the girls opens the door and exclaims

'Ivy you've got a young man! Bring him in!' They'd been drinking all day and were all in their nightdresses ready to go to bed.

'No, no' Ivy protested, 'He's gotta go back.' Despite this they hauled me in. I didn't know whether I was scared or excited."

"Several hours later eventually they let me go and I got back to the guard gate but they'd changed the guard at midnight." This new guard was far less swayed by any festive spirit. "He questioned me 'who are you? What are you doing?'

I said 'I've just seen Ivy Wilson, y'know number so and so, back to her billet.'

'What? A young whipper snapper like you? Out with one of our WAAFs?'

I said 'No!' 'I just spent Christmas day with her.'

"So the guard got his mate and ordered him to 'ring up the guard room and send out a jeep.' These two military policemen come out on the jeep, bundled me into it and took me to the guard room. I had to explain everything to the officer in charge. Eventually he turned to the other chaps with the jeep and said 'go down to hut so and so and bring Ivy

Wilson up here.'

If fourteen year old John had in fact been a German spy, he was a very convincing one. Even so the protocols and discipline of military officers demanded the entire rigmarole continue. John explains, "Ivy was brought up there too and had to explain everything in her nightdress. The officer finally concluded the matter with orders to 'take this little bugger back to the main gate, kick him up the arse and don't you come here any more.'

"By the time I got home it was about two o clock in the morning. Mother had gone to bed but father was still up." John recalls his mother Ethel always being the more authoritative and strict parent of the two. There may have been some relief on realising she was asleep upon his return but on this occasion Alfred cut him no slack either.

'Where the bloody hell have you been boy? You've been up to mischief with that young lady haven't you?'

I said 'No!'

'I don't believe you! You've been up to mischief with her!'

I said 'I-I haven't!' John admits in retrospect "It crossed my mind. I could've been up to mischief with three or four of those in the Nissen hut."

About four weeks passed under the weight of these accusations and the Perry family didn't see any sign of Ivy after the Christmas incident.

"I was right!" exclaimed John's father. "She's not coming here any more, you interfere-"

"I didn't!" John protested but ultimately it fell on deaf ears.

Eventually Ivy turned up at Raven's Cottage, full of apologies and explained "I've been confined to the barracks for a month for bringing an undesirable onto the airfield."

"Ooh, what a relief." thought John at last.

The vestiges of these airfields and bases today are a smattering of grain stores around and within crop fields. Although some of the buildings seem relatively unchanged from the forties with the distinctive semi-cylindrical roofing still visible.

When he wasn't being smuggled into women's Nissen huts, John partook in the Sunday church choir at Little Easton church. He remembers there being a rota as to who would go and operate the pumps to provide wind power to the organ.

John also joined a sports club called "The Barn Boys Club.", aptly located in a barn in Easton next to Little Easton Manor. They practised a variety of sports but John took on a fondness for football and so later progressed to Easton and Duton Hill Football Club. The club was actually comprised of players from three local villages; Little Easton, Great Easton and Duton Hill.

Here he played for several seasons, usually in a middle or left wing position and went on to win the cup in 1950. John even recalls his individual efforts, scoring two goals in the semi-final and one in the forementioned final.

Teenage John pictured here at the back on the far left.

In our talks with John, certain memories brought forth the imagery of a baby girl being pushed in a pram nestled on top of dead rabbits. In trying to explain how this came about I feel a lot of context is first needed.

By the time John's sister Judy was born in 1946, John, being the eldest, was exempt from undergoing the billeting process again. He instead kept working with his father on the farm. John recalls his father's pastime of hunting rabbits with the use of tamed ferrets, often just called "ferreting." John would accompany his father on some of these outings and eventually inherit the hobby himself.

Back in those days before the mass perpetual stocks of supermarkets, Alfred would catch and kill these wild rabbits, then clean them before handing them over to Ethel to take into town to sell to the butchers. Initially the rabbit hunting was Alfred's way of helping during wartime rationing, alongside growing his own vegetables, which a young John would assist him with. Even after the war though a bit of extra money was always helpful and Ethel would go straight from the butchers to do the food shopping.

The baby Judy would necessarily accompany Ethel on these trips and John remembers the sight of the pair. "She'd got this great big pram with a partition across and a big well underneath, an old fashioned pram. Put the rabbits in the bottom there, Judy on top and went to Dunmow to the butchers." Something that might well cause bystanders to call the police today, was routine back in the 1940's. There was no option to separate all these elements within the comfort and space of a car so this was simply how it was done.

In these early days on the farm when much of the work relied on straightforward manpower, John also remembers a less than straightforward man employed there. Nicknamed "Gaggets" (exact spelling unknown) due to his heavy smoking and retching. So fierce was his habit that "he would always cadge fags off the other men." This became incessant enough that John and his brother Peter got quite tired of this freeloading and decided to prank him.

Filling the cigarettes with horse manure, weed seed and a tooth from a comb, they distributed them amongst a couple of the other men who were in on the joke. When Gaggets inevitably came scrounging and hassled them for a smoke, they offered him one of these prank fags instead which he happily and obliviously took.

Upon lighting it, the cigarette exploded into a huge cloud of smoke with the only evidence of Gaggets remaining being a storm of coughing and swearing from somewhere within the smog. Incredibly, it took an absence of vomiting and falling for the same trick later that same day before Gaggets finally gave up asking the other farmworkers for cigarettes.

Such levity was likely a welcome and necessary relief from the long hours and high stamina demands of their daily work. John talks about the entire barns he would fill with wheat or barley sheaves bundled and tied into stacks or sometimes called "stooks". I checked this was an actual term and not just someone saying "stacks" with an accent. This process eventually becoming expedited by dedicated and automated baler machines or chaff cutters if the straw was instead intended to be used for cattle feed.

From the early days of horse and cart to towed mower and thresher machines up until the introduction of sophisticated combine harvesters. John grew up alongside these technological progresses and became intensely familiar with all their workings. The combine harvester machines for example, that could cut or "harvest" the crops as well as separate or "thresh" the crop's grain from the stalk. John can still easily recall all the models of combines over his many decades of work.

Well there's several red combines, Massey Harris, International Harvester, that was another red one. And then you've got yellow ones that were Bamford Combines. And then you've got through to these green ones, the John Deere and they're all the rage nowadays John Deere."

If we're in the habit of imagining combine harvesters, you probably picture the large modern metal-teethed behemoths. Free-standing and independently running with a driver's cabin far above all the moving parts. John however recalls some of the first combine harvesters Humphrey Trembath introduced that still needed to be towed by a tractor.

"There'd be a chap on the tractor towing the combine and the likes of meself or somebody on the combine sacking up the corn. You'd tie these sacks up, eighteen stone of wheat or barley and then you used to let them go down the slide from the combine onto the field.

A stock image example of the kind of machines John would be working on back when he started in the 1940's and 50's.

"And then the next morning, when the dew was still on, you couldn't combine until the dew went off, you had to go around picking these sacks up and take them to the barn or wherever...Corr that was hard work. Eighteen stone! I used to have them on me back and think nothing of it. Corr, couldn't do it nowadays."

Not just strenuous and exhausting but sometimes outright dangerous. John remembers hearing about and even witnessing multiple injuries and accidents befalling his poor father across his long career.

"The first one he had, he'd got this tractor. Climbed on and was setting up when...I dunno, something went wrong underneath or he was doing an adjustment and the tractor shifted while on a slope. The tractor suddenly moved and trapped him.

That was at the beginning of the last war so the army were on manoeuvres nearby, you know training and that around the area, and they spotted him. Thankfully he was crying out for help and the army went and helped move the tractor off of him." A frightening situation as Alfred was on his own in this instance.

Another anecdote involved the more immediate danger of a gale force wind and some heavy barn doors. A moment of structural weakness coupled with Alfred's preoccupied focus on his work rather than the weather, resulted in one of these heaving great doors swinging open suddenly, "and that clobbered him" John recalls.

The instances where John himself was present were arguably even more dangerous. "We'd each got a week's holiday, me and me dad. We were working on the farm and we were desperate for firewood in those days.

So ol' Humphrey Trembath said 'You go up into High Wood and get some wood if you like.'

So we went up there with a cross-cut saw and an axe and everything. We'd been up there about an hour I suppose and dad accidentally put the axe into his leg. Of course over he went, he couldn't move.

Bloody hell, what am I going to do now? I thought. All that way from Highwood." For reference, John and Alfred were currently about three miles from Raven's Farm, deep within a forest and with nothing as simple as a mobile phone or even any landlines close by back then.

"I ran right back down to the farm." John recalls.

John fetched his brother Peter and they grabbed a small tractor and trailer with some bales of straw on the latter. Together they hurried back to High Wood and managed to move the wounded Alfred onto the trailer. They drove him right through the town centre to Dunmow surgery.

"People that were walking through the town said 'Oh look, that poor man! That poor man!' while me and Pete got our arms around him and were lugging him into the surgery." Despite trailing straw all over the doctor's surgery, Alfred was seen to quickly and effectively stitched up. "We got him home and we never did get no firewood."

The final and most fraught of Alfred's near-misses came whilst working down at Easton Farm. "Corr that could've killed him." John remembers with a noticeable chilling reverence his voice. The gravity of the situation still readily apparent and potent to him all these years later.

We were tipping a load of corn in the barn there. You know, tip the trailer up and when the corn was out, let the trailer down. For some reason or other, me dad had got a broom and was sweeping away around the trailer.

He didn't realise the trailer was coming down and between the chassis and the top of the trailer, there's about that much gap. (John indicates with his fingers the very narrow size of the gap) Got his head trapped in there."

John pauses for a moment in the retelling. "I mean if that'd had gone any lower, that'd have crushed his head to bits. We rushed to the tractor, me and Peter and put the handle so that the trailer went up again. Both his ears were cut about but apart from that, he got away with that."

It's hard to say if Alfred was particularly unlucky to be finding himself in these situations or lucky that they didn't inflict any serious or lasting damage. John theorises that the worst they did was make his already failing sense of hearing slightly worse each time.

Comparatively John scraped by fairly unscathed in the farm work. For years after the war ended, unexploded bombs would occasionally be found, especially as the old aerodrome was demolished and excavated into farmland and crop fields. John remembers an expert being brought to the site of one suspected explosive.

They advised that none of the locals go near the device, which was a pointlessly late warning as John, Peter and the others involved had been handling it since they discovered it. Working onboard the tractor, John's heart would skip a beat every time a metal clank or bump passed underneath the wheels but mercifully nothing ever followed these scares

One early morning at around fifteen years old John did break his arm threshing and baling during the haymaking season. This was during som temporary work at Buildings Farm which could have played into John's unfamiliarity or nerves leading to the injury.

He was rushed to the same and likely only doctor's surgery in Dunmow as his father was. Seen to by the trustworthy Doctor Geoffrey Owen Barber, or "Dr. Gob" as he became known to the Perrys. John was actually the first baby Dr Gob delivered when he started his practice so he was a close and useful connection to have to the family. John's injury resulted in about six to seven weeks off work. Despite the doctor's order he didn't let it stop him playing football, through sly concealment of the injury.

His work on the farm and time at social clubs occupied John up until the age of twenty. During this time, a chance encounter with a pair of sodden strangers would prove a pivotal moment in the direction of his life. "After finishing football on a Saturday. I used to cycle into Dunmow with my mate Ron, Ronnie Grout, to go to the Kinema." John recounts.

While near-universally known as cinema today, in the first half of the twentieth century many establishments would go by the term "Kinema" from the initial patent of the film camera in 1891 where the device was called the "Kinetograph" or "Kinetoscope."

Also of note is a World War One memorial in Little Easton village opposite The Stag pub. Amongst others, this memorial honours the names of both a Private John James Perry and Private Rupert Charles Grout. I was unable to confirm whether these men were any relation to John or his mate Ronnie but it was an interesting aside to stumble upon.

John continues. "We'd park our bikes at a friends house and walk through the town to the Kinema, which was on the far side of town. One evening the heavens opened and it poured with rain so we ran to the nearest shop doorway for shelter where these two girls already were. We learnt their names were Jean Cook and Yvonne Garrett."

"Jean had plenty to say for herself." John remarks, recalling their first conversation.

'Where are you blokes off to?'

'Oh.' we said, 'We're going to the Kinema.'

'We can't afford to go to a Kinema' they said, 'we're still at school. We're just going around the town, window-shopping.'

"We said 'no problem, we'll take you." and the girls agreed. "Who's going with who?'

Before I could say I wanted to go with Yvonne, Yvonne herself put forward the preference 'I'd like to go with John.'

Unfortunately despite the random luck of their meeting, the downpour proved to be relentless that evening. Yvonne and Jean ended up having to tell them 'We can't go with you to the Kinema tonight 'cause we have to be in by ten o clock.' Undeterred, the boys countered.

'No problem. We'll take you tomorrow night.'

"So we walked them home down the Chelmsford Road and found that they lived next door to each other. So for several weeks we went as a foursome." Things seemed to be going well and there was a mutual interest blossoming between John and Yvonne.

"One Saturday, after football I said to Ron 'Meet you at the bottom of Park Road as usual tonight.'

'No' he said, 'I'm not going. I don't like that Jean.'

Apparently not requiring any further explanation John simply asked

'Well have you told her?'

"No!" Ron stated very definitively. "Are you going to see Yvonne?'

"Yeah" replied John, slowly realising the predicament he was being left in. He added "...Well you might've told me.'

As they lived next door to each other, I parked my bicycle outside Yvonne's. The window opened next door and Jean poked her head out first.

'Where's Ron tonight? Is he ill?'

I said 'No, he's alright.'

'Well where is he?'

John reluctantly opened the can of worms foisted on him by Ron. 'He didn't want to see you any more.'

John pauses in his recollection with a simple but telling expression of "Oh dear." Which seemed to aptly summarise the earache Ron left him with that day.

"She started moaning and groaning and then Yvonne was in her doorway, heard what was going on and said 'We'd better get going John or else we'll be late for the Kinema.' John was no doubt grateful for Yvonne's rescue at this point.

"Well that was my first night alone with just Yvonne like. Saturday night was" John pauses, "So uh, I kissed her goodnight and said 'see you

Tuesday' which was our next day for the Kinema.

Yvonne suggested 'Would you like to come down to tea tomorrow and meet mum and dad?'

'Well have you asked them?' came John's nervous reply.

'Nah' she said 'That'll be alright.'

Oof, I couldn't sleep that night."

With Ron's shirking of courtship responsibility and Yvonne's brave certainty regarding unannounced dinner guests it seems John's reputation for mischief did not leave him immune to ending up in awkward situations himself.

John resumes his story from after that sleepless night of trepidation.

"I needn't have worried because we hit it off very well. By this time Yvonne had left school and got a job at Barclays bank. She'd been there a few weeks and she said to me one evening

'I dunno how you're gonna take this but I've got to go down to Surrey, to a college for training with regards to my job at the bank.

"The Barclays bank staff are meeting me at Liverpool Street Station along with other girls and young lads for training.' John was likely dismayed to hear this but wasn't one to let it show.

'I'll write to you.' John reassured her.

"Well this was the Sunday when I'd see Yvonne off. By the Tuesday I'd got a letter from her. And we kept exchanging letters from then on. After about three weeks, I had a letter come saying she'd got the day off and that I could come up to London on the Saturday to visit."

"Normally I worked on a Saturday so I took the day off and met her up at London Bridge Station. We went for a boat trip on the Thames, then had something to eat and we was walking around London when we went by this theatre. 'corr that looks good, that what's on there.' Yvonne remarked.

So I said 'well let's go.'

'But I have to be in by midnight.' cautioned Yvonne. Despite this they chanced seeing the production.

"Afterwards Yvonne said 'I'm worried about you catching your last train back.'

'Can you come out tomorrow?' John asked.

'Well I'm allowed out between nine and six. But what are you going to do tonight?'

"This was late June, early July" so the light rolled in earlier those mornings. The college was close to Wallington Park so John decided to wait out the rest of the night there. He told Yvonne 'I'll go sit on a bench for a couple to three hours.'

He tried to sleep but couldn't catch a wink. "At about four o clock in the morning a policeman goes riding along the cycle track through the park. When he saw me he glared at me but thankfully just carried on."

"Two hours later an old boy comes from the opposite direction on a bike, stops and starts rolling a cigarette in front of me. 'Alright mate?' he said,

I said 'Yeah.'

'I bet you've got a young lady at the college don't ya?'

'What makes you think that?'

'Seen it all before' he claimed. 'I'm the caretaker at the college...I bet you could do with a cup of tea and a brush up. I've got my own little room there, come with me.'

So I went with him and he made me tea. We had a few chats and in between he'd go off on and do his duties. At nine o clock, Yvonne came out and we spent the rest of the day going around London."

"When Yvonne got back home, her father had told the bank manager that he wouldn't let Yvonne get married until she was twenty one. She was only sixteen at the time and they didn't have married women in the bank in those days."

This was effectively telling Yvonne's employer she was guaranteed to remain working for them for five more years, as the prospect of marriage often meant impending resignation for working women. This antiquated practice of terminating women's employment upon marriage was known as the "Marriage Bar."

The reasoning was that married women were supported financially by their husbands and unmarried women would be more reliable and undistracted by family obligations. Notably these restrictions eased during war time when there was no other option to fill job roles due to most men fighting overseas. That precedent perhaps helped start to erode the tradition from more and more professions until the practice was finally made illegal in the UK in 1975.

Back in the forties though, all this meant to John and Yvonne was a frustrating obstacle in their relationship and a half-decade delay on their engagement.

Yvonne asked John 'Would you be prepared to wait?' John remembers his confident reassurance at the time. 'Yeah, of course.' but privately I thought, five years. That's a long old while."

After four years Yvonne told John 'I've had a word with father' And to their delight she had persuaded him to "jack it in" in regards to the five year deal and so the pair got married at St. Mary's Church in Dunmow on the 26th March 1955. Yvonne was twenty at this time and John twenty four.

John reminisces on the event, remarking that everything went mercifully smoothly. The closest to any issues was that the vicar of Dunmow was ill at the time but the vicar of nearby Stebbing came in as substitute and performed the service.

Similarly John's best man Arthur Needham had to travel from Brentwood to Dunmow and John remembers fearing traffic delays "Oh I was sweating that he wouldn't get there in time." but thankfully in the end there was no problem here either.

John initially attempted to ask Ronnie Grout to be his best man but his response was "Well I'm not capable of doing that." It's unclear if it was fear that prompted this reply or logistics as John recalls Ronnie being in either the army or navy around this time and so preoccupied or away a lot.

It wouldn't be unheard of though for someone facing the threats of military life every day to suddenly buckle when faced with a role requiring sentimentality and sincerity. Purely speculation here on my part, but amusing speculation nonetheless.

Arthur's wife Peggy was one of Yvonne's bridesmaids alongside Yvonne's sisters Pat, Carol and Gillian. As Yvonne was one of the leaders of the local Brownies, her title being that of "Tawny Owl, the girl group also attended to provide the guard of honour.

From left to right: Alfred, Ethel, Geoffrey, Arthur, Peter, John, Yvonne, Peggy, Pat, Daisy, Fred and in the front row: Judy, Carol, Gillian and Antony (One of Yvonne's brothers).

"We had the reception at the Saracen's Head Hotel in Dunmow and when the taxi came to take us to Bishop's Stortford, where we were due to catch a train to go on honeymoon, Old Fred (Yvonne's father) said 'Oh you ain't going yet" and told the taxi bloke to come back in a couple of hours time. We didn't like it but well...you know what he is. So we got down to Eastbourne a bit late."

When finally free of the tiring social pleasantries of the event, John and Yvonne took their week-long honeymoon in Eastbourne, a pleasant coastal resort town, east of Brighton. To this day it retains a lot of early twentieth century and Victorian era landmarks and hotels, in which John and Yvonne likely spent their time, between that and the beaches.

Thanks to John's saved time off they spent a second week's vacation at a tied cottage Humphrey Trembath rented out to John. The rent was ten shillings a week, which is about fifty pence in today's money, although obviously worth a lot more back then. John and Yvonne spent this second week decorating and furnishing the cottage ready for their married life together.

The cosy but decently sized cottage came with low wooden beam ceilings across a living room, lounge, bathroom and narrow scullery towards the back of the house. A cast iron Rayburn cooker and fire was the house's only source of heating. The upstairs three Dormer bedrooms were built into the eaves of the house and the garden was far smaller in those days before its gradual expansion.

What would later become a chicken run was the primary vegetable patch at first and initially there was no driveway into the property. Instead a ditch and hedgerow with a simple wooden gate at the far end. The cottage stood alongside only a few neighbouring buildings in those days but has become less and less secluded as construction rises up in the surrounding areas.

rather than finding rows of houses opposite, the view from the living room window looks past a once quiet road leading into Dunmow town, across a horizon of numerable vast fields. John remembers these fields starting as pasture for a dairy farm before later becoming the crop fields as they stand today. This cottage at 31 Parsonage Downs would be John's home from then on into the 2020's where it is now a listed building.

These two photos show the property in recent years around 2019.

In the decade following them first moving in, Humphrey Trembath passed away and Raven's Farm was taken over by his nephew Bob Trembath. John's father Alfred still worked on the farm and John's brother Peter had now started alongside them. "By this time the farm was getting well mechanised." John recalls. "Staff were cut down to three or four".

The early smaller tractors and machinery gradually gave way to more sophisticated, larger contraptions. This peaked in later years, John remembers, when "Bob Trembath bought this massive John Deere tractor from America. I was given the job of using it on all the cultivations on nearly a thousand acres. Working very long hours".

John's eldest daughter Susan and this author's mother then interjected to ask in what year this change would have begun.

"Uh...56, 57." John estimates.

"You've missed a very important part out." Sue reminds him with a chuckle.

"Yeah I know, I was just coming to that." John insists. He goes on to describe the small matter of his daughter Susan's birth on July 31st 1956. She was actually due to be born on the 24th which would have her share a birthday with John's brother Peter. Also coincidentally, the midwife shared their surname "Perry" albeit no relation.

John describes the "mad rush to Haymead's hospital in Bishop's Stortford on the bus." He pauses. "Doesn't sound right does it? I hadn't got a car then." So catching the bus was the most feasible and fastest way for them to get to the hospital. As ramshackle as the journey seems, the birth itself was safe and without incident.

John describes visiting Yvonne and the newborn Susan in the weeks afterwards. It was often around a fortnight in those days before the mother and newborn would be fit to return home. "I used to knock off work at five o clock, run up past The Oak pub and catch the bus to come to Bishop's Stortford." After several of these exhausting time-sensitive sprints John happened upon a fellow first time father by the name of Ron Owers.

Ron worked for an agricultural merchants and so would occasionally cross paths with Bob Trembath and other landowners in the hopes of selling them farming machinery and vehicles. It's unknown if John and him had met before this point or if it was simply the kindness of strangers but Ron owned a car and offered to give John a lift to the hospital. Both Susan and his own son Peter had been born around the same time. John graciously accepted and Sue remembers her and Ron's son Peter later went to the same school together.

By the birth of John and Yvonne's second daughter, the couple were older and wiser enough to have the midwife come to them instead and Diane was born at the Parsonage Downs cottage in June 1963. Another healthy and safe birth for all involved, although Sue does remember her seven year old self being afflicted with tonsillitis during this time and having to be kept away from the newborn Diane for her safety.

John would also remedy their travel limitations around this time when Humphrey's car went up for auction. Apparently very set on acquiring it at any cost except a significantly financial one, John actually used his prior knowledge of the vehicle to subtly sabotage the auction by removing the spark plugs before the showing.

As anyone with lax car maintenance can probably attest, the whipping hiss noise that is produced from a car with faulty or lacking spark plugs doesn't make for an appealing sales pitch and the car probably sounded more like an incoming helicopter than a roadworthy automobile. Having dissuaded any other buyers, John bought the car himself and quietly replaced the spark plugs once the vehicle was safely in his possession.

The car was a Morris Minor 1000 series. A very classically 50's looking car with rounded edges and a nose-like ridge along the middle of the bonnet. Yvonne passed her driving test before John but on his second attempt he succeeded and John's driving got its first real test run on a family holiday in the mid sixties.

Rockley Sands was and still is a small but popular beach with an adjacent caravan park in Poole, Dorset. Near to the village of "Hamworthy" which isn't relevant but anywhere called Hamworthy is worthy of mention to my mind. The Perry family made the long trip down to a hired caravan here and Sue unearthed the following photo of both that caravan and John's dubiously won car at the time.

Both John and Sue recall the car's number plate etched permanently in their memory.

It was a holiday looked back on fondly with John and Yvonne enjoying the weather and the beach while looking after Diane who was still in a pushchair at this point. Sue remembers her young self building sandcastles and playing on the nearby swings. She doesn't recall anyone venturing into the sea or at the very least not herself as she hadn't learnt to swim yet.

John, Sue and Diane alongside the caravan and Humphrey's old car.

The park has expanded considerably since those days and I imagine the caravans now include in-built toilets which wasn't true at the time of John's trip. John and his family would enjoy several other seaside holidays around this time at locations like Camber Sands and day trips out to Clacton-on-sea.

John and his brother-in-law at the time Keith Brown, in a lively game on the beach at Clacton-on-sea.

In the colder winter months John still kept warm memories of spirited and lively festive seasons with his family. They would buy a genuine Christmas tree every year without fail and when these became scarce John remembers travelling to Broxted with his brother Peter to chop one down themselves.

This was not without danger however as one recollection tells of Peter climbing to the top of a sizeable tree and hacking away at the tip with a pen knife. John's description told me this was to "level it" but I failed to get elaboration on what exactly that means. My best guesses are either fashioning a holding for decoration atop the tree or simply shortening the tree in order to fit it inside the house.

Regardless Peter's efforts to cut short the tree were cut short themselves when he lost purchase and fell onto another tree laid below it. What the tree lessened in distance fell, the uneven surface made worse for a painful landing. Peter has since fully recovered but John remembers some complaints of considerable back pain for a time after.

Amateur lumberjacking hazards aside, the Christmas days were merry and sociable affairs. The Perry family would often travel to Yvonne's parents where her mother Daisy Garrett would cook a traditional Christmas dinner. Boxing day would then bring everyone to Parsonage Downs. John recalls getting a snooker table for the front room which with the combined children of both families resulted in a packed and bustling room full of relatives and revelry.

The nights would end with Yvonne's father Fred and John drinking, playing cards and betting money long into the early morning. John remembers these games of Pontoon and Blackjack quite fondly. Perhaps more fondly than Fred did as the tendency was for John to win "quite severely."

On one occasion John and Fred were accompanying their games with some kind of strong liqueur until four in the boxing day morning. This robbed John of the foresight to remember he had agreed to go and play football for Easton that day. As hungover as he felt, let history show that he did manage to attend the match, though in what state we can only imagine. John himself left the summary at **"rough."**

John settled into a comfortable life at Parsonage Downs. He continued working at Raven's Farm and spending time with his new family. With television becoming a more common household fixture John enjoyed many an evening watching Benny Hill and Dick Emery comedy shows. Sue remembers buying him a Benny Hill record as a present one year.

Sue also recalls some fond and poignant memories growing up around this time. Ethel bringing her water for the China tea sets she used to play with in the garden. The abandoned WW2 military pillbox near Raven's Cottage where Sue used to venture into and that still stands to this day.

Taken in June 2022. It's since had the entrance blocked off but you can still peer in through the loopholes (windows).

Later there were trips to a Chelmsford theatre where John, Sue and Alfred would watch live wrestling. Sue can still conjure the amusing sight of "old Alf" getting so immersed and animated in the audience, gesticulating wildly with his walking stick. Thankfully the ceilings were out of his reach this time.

She also remembers that they must all be deathly quiet to hear the football results on TV of a Saturday afternoon. John would later take Sue to see several enjoyable live football matches with his friend Roy Short. Less enjoyable was the car sickness and cramped conditions in grandad Fred's grey Vauxhall car. As all of the Garrett family and all of the Perrys crammed inside this one vehicle to travel on seaside outings.

Another memory (or lack thereof) was when John solidified that football should remain his chosen sport. Playing tennis out in the garden with Sue, a missed racket swing collided instead with his own head and he "laid himself out" to use his own words.

John recalls Yvonne springing into action telling him "Hold on a minute, don't pass out yet. I'll go and get the smelling salts" but John did in fact pass out briefly. "Too late, I'd gone." He retells. "I reckon I must've hit a nerve just above the eye or somewhere."

Not quite following in Alfred's footsteps but John did narrowly brush with danger on several other occasions. During the busy harvest season one year, John developed a painful hernia and could no longer work. Bob Trembath didn't want him taking too much time off and so he paid for a private doctor who performed the operation in John's front room.

The operation was successful but grisly and Diane remembers hiding up in her bedroom until it was all over. Yvonne recalls that John claimed blood stains from the event could be seen for years afterwards although she personally believes they were just stains from opening beer cans.

Another tale sparks from when John once employed the use of an "Earth Auger". A kind of ground drill used for boring holes to be fitted with uninteresting fences or lamp posts. As the rotating drill descended, John was oblivious to the flashing light show he embroiled the surrounding neighbourhood into. All the nearby bungalows and plaster cottages flashed intermittently as their power cut off and then on again repeatedly.

Before any baffled and blinded residents could approach John about the issue, John stopped the machine and decided to dig the last depths of the hole manually with a shovel. Striking down into what he thought was solely dirt and earth, he instead struck the main power cable and engulfed the entirety of Little Easton village in darkness.

An electrician from the National Grid eventually arrived at the scene of the blackout and assessed that if John hadn't been wearing his rubber wellington boots, he'd have been reduced to a pile of ash.

John recounts another tale from working on the farm that is either far less dramatic and death-defying or the most dangerous encounter of all, depending on your disposition to certain beef products. John and Peter would report to Bob Trembath at the farmhouse at eight o clock every morning to receive their orders for the day.

And every day Bob would talk for a long time with seemingly no concern for them actually starting work. He would also always make them a cup of Bovril. The obscenely salty beef extract paste that is both banned in the United States and blurs the line between drinkable liquid and condiment spread.

Bob's quirks didn't help matters here as his drinks were made so thick that the spoon stood up free-standing within it with both John and Peter hating and dreading the ritual offering from their boss. At the back of the house where this beef briefing took place, there was a short L-shaped passage to the back door.

John and Peter devised a strategy whereupon they used to take it in turns to throw the Bovril across the back lawn whenever Bob wasn't looking. They were never caught in this self-preservation endeavour but Bob couldn't understand why a certain strip of the lawn grew much taller than the rest.

One day as it landed on John's turn to launch the Bovril out the door. He went to throw the cup and it broke off at the point of greatest momentum. Flying off down the garden and leaving John with only a severed ceramic handle in his grip. John reported the occurrence back to Bob in a truncated non-incriminating revision.

"I've had a slight accident." John told him.

"No problem." said Bob, unfazed. "I'll make you another one."

One of John's most enduring and large scale accomplishments came as part of the crew responsible for excavating an entire reservoir. Roughly sometime in the sixties, by Peter's estimate, the brothers worked with diggers and their bare hands to prepare the enormous lakebed on Laundry Lane just off from Park Road.

About three and a half acres in size and between fifteen and eighteen feet deep. To this day you can see the fully formed reservoir as a roadside view and a popular fishing spot for carp. John recalls that most of the trees bordering it are ones he planted all those years ago.

The reservoir in July 2023

By the end of the seventies multiple contributing factors made it necessary for Alfred and Ethel to move out from Raven's Farm to a bungalow on Woodview Road in Dunmow. They were somewhat cautious about leaving, having been attached to Raven's Farm for half a century at this point.

There were upsides however such as being closer to their daughter Judy and Raven's was not left in unfamiliar hands as Peter continues to live and work there to this day.

John remembers being the designated removal man that day. "I picked this van up and I was backwards and forwards. Peter helped me load it that end but he didn't come with me and then Michael (Judy's husband) was at the other end. Yeah, a busy old day that was." Sue also remembers a lot of their old furniture being handed down to her as she had just moved house as well in her first marriage.

Apparently the bungalow was not Alfred and Ethel's first choice as they found John and Yvonne's home at Parsonage Downs very appealing and time would prove they wouldn't be the last to become envious of the property.

But put simply, John and Yvonne had no desire to move out and more practically, with the passing of time, it was now a busy and dangerous main road for Alfred to travel to work on, equipped as he was with nothing more than an old push-bike.

Despite being in his mid seventies, it was only after this move that Alfred fully retired. While not working full time in these later years, he had remained gainfully employed at Raven's farm for sixty two years. A feat that was recognised in the local papers shortly after their move.

In the 1980's Bob Trembath shook up arrangements after years of growing crops at Raven's Farm. He started hiring contractors to do the mainline farming work and moved to Little Easton farm instead, taking three corn fields of about thirty acres and repurposing them to make an enormous garden. John remembers the hundreds of trees, shrubs, roses and other plants he had sown and how a lot of them were then transferred from Raven's to the new house.

Bob had a pavilion built at Easton Farm with a swimming pool, jacuzzi, tennis and croquet courts. He also had the grain barn turned into a large garden room growing tropical plants, holding wedding receptions and various other functions. Such a massive upheaval to a well-worn routine might have provoked some anxiety in John but he was never the type to let it show.

John recounts that "Bob took lots of holidays abroad, mainly to Tenerife where he owned a fabulous villa. I often took him and his lady friend to the airport at either Stansted or Luton. Later on I was given a two week holiday in Tenerife. I took my sister Judy, her husband Michael and their daughter Anna.

We went up Mount Teide." John recalls. An active volcano and the third tallest in the world. Thankfully it hasn't erupted since 1909. He reminisces fondly saying "I had many lovely holidays with my family. Italy, Greece, the Greek islands, Spain, Lanzarote and nearer home, Guernsey and Scotland." Whilst holidaying at the aforementioned, John actually managed to impress the Scottish locals with his endurance in being able to drink neat whiskey.

Meanwhile, less flatteringly at Halkidiki in Northern Greece, he had been convinced of the virtues of the plant Witch-hazel as more effective than sun cream in the boiling over thirty degree heat. John's daughter Diane advised him against this, stating it to be more specifically an after-sunburn treatment and not a preventative block. Unfortunately John was adamant and later got so sunburnt he couldn't even walk. Diane claims a few days later he shed his entire skin like a snake.

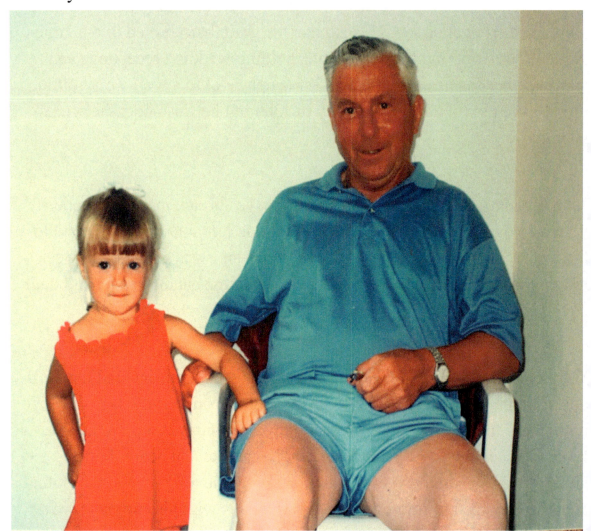

A toasty-looking John with his first granddaughter Laura.

Personally I can recall my grandad John on many of our holidays growing up. Despite being in his later years, he managed tremendous inclines up steep Spanish hills and having no doubt learnt from the witch-hazel incident, managed far better than I in the sweltering heat as we rode a camel together in Lanzarote 2007.

In sharp contrast to these sunny memories was John's foray into the "glamorous" world of filmmaking or perhaps an experience better described as a media mudslide. "Around Easton Manor they were filming a gangster film called The Fear." he recounts. "The middle of July but atrocious weather. The fields were completely waterlogged."

A woman named Liz Kerry approached John and said they were unable to get the lorries across the fields and what she needed was a man with a tractor and trailer. "So we okayed it with Bob and she asked me to report to the manor house at eight o clock on the Thursday morning, leaving my tractor by the church.

When I reported for duty Liz said 'Come along in John and I'll tell you what I want you to do over breakfast.'

I said 'I've already had breakfast.'

'I'm sure you could eat another one'

It started pouring with rain and Liz asked 'Have you got waterproofs with you?'

'No, but I've got some at home.'

'Where do you live?'

I said 'Dunmow.'

'I'll take you home to get them after breakfast.' She concluded.

John remembers speeding along with Liz in her little red sports car when she told him she had been in the Dunmow area for a couple of days and fallen in love with a cottage nearby. "I'll show it to you along the way." she said. As they approached Parsonage Downs John had to say "Slow down, we're almost there. This is where I live."

"And this is the cottage I have fallen for." Liz revealed. "I would love to look around it sometime when I'm not busy."

The filming took them back and forth between Dunmow and Little Easton across several days and nights. John was working alongside his brother Peter and six lorry drivers all transporting equipment, props and sets. John tells how one of the last bits of filming took place on a busy Friday afternoon around The Doctor's Pond in Dunmow and afterwards Liz took John and the others to the Chequers pub for a well-deserved meal and drinks.

Rather than a hearty send off however, John and the crew then had to travel back to Little Easton for more filming throughout the night until about four in the Saturday morning. Even by John's high endurance standards this was a hectic and unrelenting pace.

"There was a rush to get all the scenery, etc back to the lorries. Liz told me to report to the manor house and she would pay me. Confused, I said 'you've already paid me.' During my three days with Euston Films on several occasions Liz would put bank notes in my pocket.

'Those were only tips.' she stated. This rather upset the lorry drivers as they were all employed by her on a weekly wage. One of them said

'I think she fancies you mate. Do you fancy her?'

'No way.' I said.

I went to the manor house to be paid and Liz said I was wonderful. 'We could not have done it without your tractor and trailer. We hope to come back again sometime as we like this area. I will come back in a few weeks to pay Bob Trembath. Thank you so much, you must be exhausted. I bet your wife will make a fuss of you when you get home.'

Some weeks later Bob came up the garden and said 'the lady from Euston Films has been to pay me. She said 'you were fantastic with what you did.' You better have the money she gave me. She wanted to see you but I said that you were abroad on holiday.'

Even though this sounds like a convenient excuse to avoid Liz's cloying media patter and threats of home invasion, John was genuinely abroad at this time though he can't recall where. Despite the property envy and the bedraggled swampy nature of the work, John can't help but look back fondly on the intensely profitable experience.

"I did alright out of that, I was hoping they'd come back but of course the manor changed hands you see. The people that were there moved out and others came in but I mean they were fantastic that filming. I'd got roughly about five hundred quid for sort of two and a half, three days."

The Fear eventually became a five episode TV series in 1988 starring Iain Glen, Susannah Harker and Jerome Flynn, among others. Looking online I found screenshots of Iain Glen and Anthony Valentine in Easton Manor grounds as well shots with Little Easton Church visible in the background. This is where John parked his tractor each day before starting work. John now has a book adaptation of the series as well.

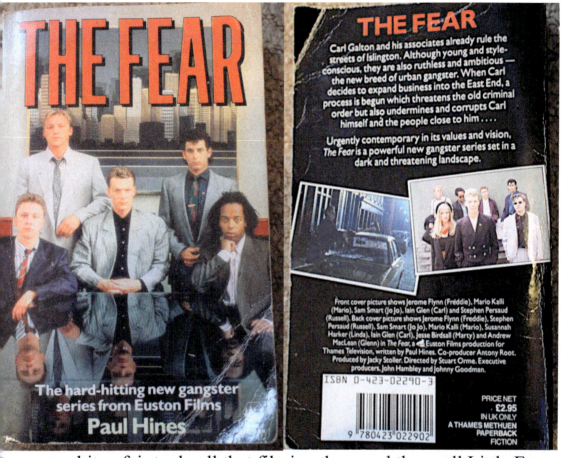

t seems a bit unfair to do all that filming there and then call Little Easton "a dark and threatening landscape." But that's media types for you.

Another background brush with fame for John came from the aforementioned church. Jack Filby was a reverend at Little Easton who amongst his claims to fame was previously being a manager for Cliff Richard, as well as the equally impressive connection of having christened this author. By the late eighties, John and Jack knew each other fairly well as one of John's jobs was to mow the grass around the rectory.

John recounts him playing his guitar in church and even holding several pop concerts around the church and the manor across the road. He would come to be known as "the rocking reverend" and was a much loved local figure. John remembers a conversation where Jack expressed a desire for more varied kinds of public events "I think we need something different, can you think of anything?" to which John replied confidently,

"Revive the Countess Of Warwick Show."

Jack was relatively new to the area and had never heard of this so John explained. Originally a flower and garden show in the latter half of the 1800's, the titular Countess Frances Evelyn Greville (or "Daisy" if you're short on time) expanded the event with sporting activities and horticultural marquees. The late-Victorian philanthropist died at Little Easton Lodge in 1938, when John was just a boy but despite this John learned of the old events and they struck a chord with his horticultural sensibilities.

The Reverend liked the idea and agreed to move forward with it so John got in contact with a man called Alan Prior. Alan worked as a gardener for the Countess Of Warwick at Easton Lodge. Preparations were made to bring the show back culminating in a successful reopening in September 1990.

"So together, myself, Jack, Alan and his wife started the show with a horticultural marquee, where people could exhibit vegetables, fruit, flowers, floral art, cookery, handicrafts and many other things. The show has since expanded to two days over the August bank holiday with dog shows, horse shows, vintage cars, ploughing and it attracts thousands of people each day and has been running for over thirty years."

An impressive achievement to have helped originate but only the start of several recognitions for John that decade."At the age of sixty five I went to the Essex Show ground to receive my Long Service Award along with other farm workers."

At this time on the 22nd June 1996, John had fifty one years service as an agricultural worker. Incidentally John's father earned this same award in 1969 for roughly the same amount of years worked and John retains photos of the award being presented to Alfred by the Queen mother.

This has even been reported on in local newspapers as Alfred Perry's sixty two years work by the time he retired, combined with John's just over half century and his brother Peter's forty five years at the time of John's award, makes for an eye-catching headline of one hundred and fifty years of farm work.

The award materially consists of a certificate and a small engraved medallion which, both his own and his father's, John kept framed at home and naturally felt a great sense of pride in.

By this point Alfred and Ethel had both sadly passed away of natural causes. Alfred in 1984 at the age of eighty one and Ethel in 1992 at the age of ninety one. Towards the end of Ethel's life, some senility required Judy to visit her often and help cook, clean and care for her mother but untimely illness and an eventual kidney transplant meant that John had to take over these duties from Judy for a time.

John would complete his often long hours at work and then travel to Ethel's and help out there but ultimately this setup proved untenable and Ethel was moved into a care home called Redbond Lodge in Dunmow. She passed away during the first weekend there.

A difficult experience for anyone and impossible to prepare for. It is at least some comfort that the nineties offered John a sense of recognition and appreciation in his work and expertise. I'm sure if Alfred and Ethel had lived to see his many hard-earned commendations they would be filled with pride.

John's tireless work and generosity was recognised again in 1999 when he received a Community Award from the Uttlesford council in Saffron Walden. The award is described as "For those who have carried out outstanding work in the community." which John goes onto describe.

"Yeah, I used to put up signs and this, that and the other, and they used to call on me, "Can you do this? Can you do that?" apart from all the hours I put in on the farm."

This largely entailed John assisting others with their gardens as was his speciality but it clearly greatly endeared him to the local community. "It was Jack Filby who nominated me. Yeah, he put my name forward and everybody else agreed. I think there's a photo of me on the steps."

"Some old dear from one of the villages said "Can I hold onto your arm? I'm frightened of falling down the stairs. You won't mind, will you?"

"No, I said, carry on."

Corr if I got all the photos out, you'd be here for a couple of months I reckon."

John tells how Jack offered to drive him to the ceremony that night. "By this time Jack was in the early stages of motor neuron disease and couldn't get up to the top of the building so a young lady who worked for Uttlesford took us up in the lift. After the presentation and photographs Jack got talking to the mayor of Uttlesford who had his own Jazz band and as such we were almost the last people to leave. Jack'd had a little bit to drink but he said he was alright driving home."

Despite this assurance, the pair got into trouble as they came to a sharp bend in the road. John recalls the brakes screeching in his ears and the reverend repeating "god be with us, god be with us" as the car swerved suddenly.

"Some bugger wants to be with us!" came John's panicked reply. By divine intervention or otherwise, Jack regained control of the vehicle and the two arrived home safely, if a little shaken.

In light of all these awards it seems pertinent to wonder where exactly John got his green fingers from. Certainly some natural talent for horticulture shines through, combined with many years work and experience gained on Raven's Farm, learning from his father. John himself however, gives a great deal of the credit to Alfred's father and his grandfather, helpfully also called John Perry. "That's where I learnt my gardening, off of him."

John's grandfather actually worked for the Countess of Warwick in his time. It is likely from his grandfather that John first learnt of the titular show and its popularity as an annual event. Even as a boy before John started working with Alfred at Raven's Farm, he would assist his grandfather in the gardening by the Alms Houses opposite Little Easton Church. He learnt a great deal from him at a pivotal age for such skills becoming ingrained.

The horticultural shows in which John exhibited this lifetime of gardening expertise were a mainstay throughout his life and he became well-renowned for his prowess at winning the contests and no doubt his affable charm and humour with the other attendees.

"It kinda all started at Dunmow Horticultural Society." He retells. Before and during the Countess Of Warwick show, John had been a secretary at the Dunmow Horticultural Society for some thirty years. Providing his services on the paperwork side of things but also taking part in a committee wherein members organised the society's own exhibitions and shows.

John's speciality was his prized vegetable growing and he has a magnificent wall of awards across a lifetime of honing his craft. Occasionally dabbling in the floral section contests but primarily his assorted vegetable trays won him innumerable cups and medals. Humongous pumpkins and a "Longest Runner Bean" trophy to name but a few. "I also entered shows in some of the surrounding villages. High Easter, Bardfield and Finchingfield.

It should be noted that the rosettes continue along the entire span of the ceiling beams. Standing at the farthest end of the room, I couldn't fit them all in one photo.

John's brother Geoffrey frequently entered these shows too and John recalls one such event where any possible feelings of brotherly competitiveness would have been stoked to a blaze. There was an entry for a "Specimen Rose" and the brothers had both nurtured their single rose to be the best it could be. As they arrived at the show on the day, John was dismayed to find the stalk of his rose had broken in transit rendering the effort useless.

Geoffrey however had foreseen this possibility and had a backup secondary rose which he offered to John so as to have any entry at all. When the specimens were finally judged John went on to win first place with Geoffrey's backup rose, whereas Geoffrey himself didn't place at all.

Others in the family also took to demonstrating their skills. Geoffrey's forte was the floral and bakery sections, whereas Judy and Michael maintained heavy involvement in the Dunmow show and won many times for their floral arrangements and photography respectively.

John, Geoffrey and Judy at The Countess Of Warwick Show, mid 2000's

This show coupled with The Countess Of Warwick show meant that the Perrys were never long without some showcase on the horizon to practice and prepare for. In the future, even John's great grandchildren would enter their arts and crafts entries into the children's section of The Countess Of Warwick show.

Sue remembers in John's later life, he would start the year remarking how he wasn't going to enter any shows this time and inevitably he would find himself cultivating a winning entry by the end of it.

Another memorable tale from these shows was the sight of John dressed as a gnome at The Countess Of Warwick show. Sue remembers going with him to find such a costume and collect it from the fancy dress shop. What Sue wasn't aware of until the writing of this book was that John had been dared to undertake the getup by his neighbour, in exchange for a bottle of whiskey. With this as the prize, it's little surprise that John jumped whole-heartedly into the tomfoolery.

On the day of the show itself, nobody, not even Geoffrey, recognised the beard-stroking, bright red suited, pointy-hatted figure wandering around the stalls and marquees. John's neighbour ultimately honoured the bet with him although other offers were proposed as John took note that "a number of elderly ladies wanted to take me home to sit in their garden."

Throughout the years as John built a family for himself, he was also joined by a string of canine companions of varying sorts and temperaments. Their first dog was a Fox Terrier and noted "little sod" called Mickey. He came to them from a fox hunting group in Pelham in the early seventies. Still at a young age, it's unclear why Mickey was retired from the pack in Pelham. Perhaps it was his less than amicable attitude that caused his departure.

Immediately after Mickey passed, a West Highland Terrier named Dusty joined them. Considered more Yvonne's dog than John's but he recalls being the one present when Dusty sadly keeled over. John buried him in the garden where all his dogs ultimately would be and even some of his daughter Diane's.

Dusty was then succeeded by Lucky. A mongrel breed belonging to Sue when she came back to live with John for a couple of years. When Sue moved out again she decided to leave Lucky in John's care, as the gentle and soppy little dog had become familiar and comfortable at the Parsonage Downs cottage.

John remembers Lucky developing a fondness for riding alongside him in the tractor and he would sulk if for whatever reason he couldn't accompany him. Lucky, that is, not John. Lucky passed away due to pancreatic cancer in 1988 while Sue was pregnant with her first son.

With a clear pattern established for dog names ending in the suffix "-ey", Mickey, Dusty and Lucky were concluded with Lady, a border collie who would also join John in the tractor and on the combine harvesters as he worked through the nineties.

Lady with a collection of John's prize-winning pumpkins.

John recalls the first time he took her along on one of his Saturday morning pheasant shoots. She was unprepared for the sudden volume to erupt from the guns and was startled. "Lady belted off into the distance. called her, hunted around everywhere for her.

"Eventually I said to the others 'you carry on with the shoot and I'll keep looking" but despite his best efforts Lady was nowhere to be found after hours searching. Dismayed, John eventually had to concede the loss.

He dejectedly returned home alone only to find Lady sat patiently on the back doorstep. She had ran all the way home to Parsonage Downs from Broxted, a considerable four to five mile journey. "She must've seen in the van when I took her and knew the route to come back. I mean, crossing roads and one thing or another and there she sat on the back doorstep, I couldn't believe it."

Lady's strong instincts were less helpfully demonstrated when Sue and Diane began to bring John's grandchildren over to visit. Lady would have to be shut away in another room due to her tendency to nip at their heels in an effort to "herd" the children as if they were sheep and her the dutiful sheepdog. Lady eventually passed away one night and John came down in the morning to find her unresponsive.

John hasn't owned any dogs himself since Lady but the excitable scampering of paws was never far away in his life. Diane has owned several generations of Golden Retrievers and Sue's energetic Labrador Retriever Louis or more recently the familiar sight of a part Border Collie mix called Alfy, all loved to make use of John's expansive gardens to race around in. The latter has even occasionally interrupted the writing of this book with his doleful expressions.

Besides dogs, John has also kept tame rabbits and ferrets over the years. Perhaps more consistently than all however has been his fondness for chicken farming. He estimates he's kept chickens for the majority of his life and whenever he was absent his brother Peter could be entrusted to come and feed them for him.

For his ninetieth birthday his granddaughter Kayleigh baked him an impressive chicken cake, thankfully in shape and not ingredients. Meanwhile amongst his great grandchildren his poultry reputation has earned him the affectionate nickname "Grandad Chicken."

I remember watching him head out to feed the clucking group in between our discussions for the book. Alfy once sneakily followed him into the run but luckily there was no incident between him and the chickens so this became routine whenever we were visiting. John would also regularly offer myself and the rest of the family free and free range eggs. "It's a nice little sideline, chickens. Until the bloody fox comes and gets them."

John with his granddaughter Kayleigh and his 90th birthday chicken cake.

John also talks about the "ferreting" pastime he had picked up from his father, albeit without the added step of taking the rabbits to town in a pram. "Peter didn't seem to be interested a lot. So I had a couple of mates who used to come with me." He recalls being accompanied by both Roy Short and later his friend Basil, a retired local farm worker.

John would keep the semi-tame ferrets in cages in his garage before transporting them in suitably named "Ferret boxes". Large, often double compartmented wooden or metal containers with fastening locks. People were rightly afraid of the ferret's powerful bite but John knew how to handle them so as to avoid any injury. The ferret would be released into the burrow and then a net placed over the hole to stop the rabbit escaping.

They even had a battery powered device called a "Ferret Finder" which was essentially a collar with a radio receiver that could track the ferret's movements via a linked device. Once the ferret caught and killed the rabbit it would return out of the hole and John and the others would have to dig up the rabbit from above. This likely meant very careful watching of the tracker to ascertain where the ferret stopped and the rabbit was at the point of the kill or else a long arduous task of digging up the entire burrow.

Despite all this preparation, on one outing John and Basil were having no luck catching any rabbits. More confusingly, the Ferret Finder kept going off underneath Basil's feet. Once it was determined that Basil was neither standing above any ferrets or himself, a massive, clothed ferret in disguise, John deduced that the device was connecting on the same frequency as Basil's hearing aid.

Even after identifying the problem the pair didn't catch anything for the entirety of that day as John spent the rest of the time loudly chastising

Basil and scaring off any remaining rabbits. This tale went down a riot with other farmers and earned the pair the nickname of "The Teletubbies." It's unclear what the connection was beyond them both just being a bit silly and having unexplained audio visual transmissions but their peers went so far as to delineate Basil as "Lala" and John as "Po."

The issue of deafness and troubled hearing became increasingly prevalent in John's later life. He explained it very matter of factly as if a pervasive affliction through the family. "Yeah well it built up, like it has with me, over the years. He'd [Alfred] got a sister who was deaf, me auntie May who lived in Broxted. That seemed to build up over the years...But it's sort of inherited because I mean Geoffrey was deaf and now I've got it...Yet me grandad, he wasn't deaf."

John seemed to largely accept his own hearing difficulties, although once he had to invest in a hearing aid it was not uncommon for him to simply leave it out somewhere unworn. Which was only an issue when he forgot to put it back in once a conversation started.

The opposite problem occurred in early 2023 where advancements in miniaturisation of the technology resulted in a hearing aid getting stuck in John's inner ear. After many rescue attempts from Diane and Sue, the piece was eventually (if uncomfortably) retrieved with a pair of tiny tweezers.

Also in early 2023, John's hearing or lack thereof briefly defeated both myself and Sue during the writing of this book. In a moment that I felt was best transcribed verbatim here.

Sue begins by asking for elaboration on Alfred and Ethel's personalities.

"You said about nana being strict?" John looks at her blankly. "Nana was the strict one...Nana was the stricter one."

"Do what?" John asks.

"Nana was stricter."

"Was what?"

"Strict. Strict with you. Whereas grandad was more easy going."

John doesn't reply but looks about in confusion. Sue continues to attempt the transmission.

"Nana was strict."

John does his best to bridge the communication gap. "Was sick?"

"No, **strict.** S-T-R-I-C-T"

John says nothing but looks quizzically at his daughter.

"Bossy! Strict!" Sue can't help but laugh at this point, as I myself am smirking whilst presciently noting down the conversation.

"Ohh, I'm not with you at the moment." John concedes.

"No I know you're not." Sue jibes.

John leans over out of his chair in renewed effort. "Nana was what?"

"Strict. Bossy."

"Huh?"

Bossy! Strict!" Still no comprehension "Bloody hell."

F-I-T-C-H?" Asks John

"No! that's fight!" replies Sue, which it isn't but we'll forgive a spelling error in the exasperation of the moment.

"Huh?!"

Strict."

"Fitch?"

"NO! Oh Christ." Sue relents and fetches a notepad to write on.

"I ain't got me glasses on." John adds.

"Oh bloody hell." Sue's dog Alfy gets up and shakes, piqued by all the commotion.

"Look out Alfy." John jovially warns, chuckling to himself.

"Yeah look out Alfy" Sue repeats sarcastically, handing John his glasses. "It's not even that important either." John puts on his glasses and Sue shows him the troublesome word on the notepad.

"Where are we?" John asks, scanning the page.

"There."

"Oh strict!"

"Hooray" exclaims Sue wearily.

"...Bloody hell, not much. Corr she was strict alright." John finally answers, laughing at the entire ordeal.

Returning to the timeline back in 2010, when John reached his eightieth birthday, Judy and Michael took him to see the famous Big Band musician and composer James Last at the Royal Albert Hall. Having released over one hundred albums since the mid forties and proving hugely successful in the UK and his home country of Germany. John fondly remembers the event "That was good that was. I've got loads of tapes, loads of videos."

James Last's "happy music" as it was known, consisted of jaunty, upbeat orchestral tunes with bass and brass at the forefront. Despite his prolific presence, John was somewhat lucky to see the performer when he did as five years later Last would pass away at the age of eighty six from an undisclosed illness.

John's own battles with illness entered his life around this time as he was diagnosed with bowel cancer. With the fraught workplace hazards of his farming and the unknowable lottery of misfortune life gambles us all into, it was impressive that this was the first time in around seventy year John had needed to go to hospital.

I remember the startling effects of the surgery on John's appearance. When I next saw him, he had lost a considerable amount of weight and his face was pale and gaunt. Despite the ordeal he still greeted me with a smile and a chuckle as I routinely hit my head on the low ceilings of his living room.

Some years after his cancer operation, John was caught performing his own risky operation when he painted the front end of his house using nothing but a basic ladder for support, even at the highest points of the house.

When questioned about the safety he remarked "that ladder weren't going nowhere" because he'd tied a large rope to it with the other end trailing up through his bedroom window and around a large and hopefully very heavy wardrobe.

Evidence of him working right up until the age of ninety one came into Sue and Diane's possession after the fact in the form of a video recorded by Timothy Trembath, Bob's nephew. The video shows John and Peter pulling trailing ivy down from the walls and roof of a shed. John himself balancing precariously on the side of a trailer.

It's unclear how much John felt his age in later years but such an attitude certainly didn't suggest any caution or frailty. Not when there was gardening work that needed doing.

John's ninetieth birthday couldn't have been a more jarring contrast from the grandiosity of his eightieth. Its unfortunate placement right in the midst of the 2020 Covid-19 pandemic. This meant Sue and Diane had an uphill battle to make what arrangements they could to give John as special a day as possible. Visitation and social interaction was heavily restricted at the time but within those boundaries, a small get-together was thankfully feasible.

The whims of weather were less kind however and it was a day largely spent sheltered under a sizeable socially-distanced gazebo, as icy November rains buffeted them from all angles. I remember watching this from the relative warmth of my flat, sending my own regards digitally through the patchy signal of a Zoom call. In keeping with the restrictions on numbers, only a few close family and friends could attend but John appreciated everyone's effort given the tough circumstances.

Sadly this was not the last of the pandemic's stranglehold on everyone's lives as in July 2021 Geoffrey passed away of natural causes at his Dunmow home. As many as were permitted attended the funeral and despite John being less capable of travel in these later years, he made a point to attend the wake. His brother's absence was sorely felt at the horticultural shows when such events became feasible again.

Geoffrey's severe asthma left him with a certain physical frailty for most of his life but the man himself showed no such meekness. A professional gardener, keen motorbike enthusiast and noted ladies man, he'll be remembered for his playful demeanour and wicked sense of humour throughout his eighty nine years of life.

It was also around this time that Bob Trembath passed away at the grand old age of one hundred and one. This coupled with Geoffrey's passing was likely quite an emotional blow for John but as ever, he'd rarely let it show. For all the japes and jokes surrounding his boss, John had a great deal of respect for Bob Trembath after so many decades of loyal employment.

Despite John now being in his nineties, he was still working three days a week up until this point. Only after Bob passed did this then reduce to a few hours a week of him and Peter attending the farm for upkeep and tidying. John's unrelenting core as an industrious working man meant he wouldn't fully officially retire until March 2023 as his health began to decline.

On April 3rd 2023, John was rushed to hospital after his daughters couldn't get hold of him on the phone and became increasingly concerned. Initial fears were that the bowel cancer he successfully fough and beat twelve years prior had returned and while this proved not to be the case, John was ultimately diagnosed to be in an unrecoverable state. It was a stressful, sleepless night for Sue and Diane consulting doctors and tending to John but they never once left his side.

His sister Judy visited him the following morning, alongside her husband Michael, with Sue and Diane still right beside him. The doctors and nurses did all they could to make him as comfortable as possible and with a combination of painkillers and vitamin intakes, later that day John recovered a great deal of lucidity and charisma.

As I travelled to visit him for perhaps the last time, it was a welcome surprise to find him jovial and talkative. "How's the book going?" he asked as I approached the bed. It was an apt question as the entire taxi ride there I'd been ruminating how, if I could get across no other information to him, I wanted him to at least know the book would get finished and all the time we spent was not in vain.

I'm thankful for everyone else there during my visit, as Sue, Diane, Yvonne and all of John's grandchildren kept a light and jocular atmosphere. We all knew the situation and in those moments of silence or hesitation the solemn gravity of events did inevitably seep in. However it is testament to the good humour we all inherited from John that these moments were few and brief.

I hope that some of John's last memories are of the warmth and laughter in that room, surrounded by his family as he joked about flirting with the nurses and remarking "oh dear" or "I'm a silly old bugger aren't I?". When eventually we had to leave him in the nurse's care, it was lastly Diane, Sue and myself saying our goodbyes to him. His daughters kissed him and told him they loved him before ensuring with the nurses that they were aware and tending to him regularly.

For all my overthinking, I hadn't pre-planned and conceptualised this part and thus found myself stuttering and stumbling over my possibly final words to him. I think somewhere amidst the jumble I said "take care" and made a point to gently touch him on the arm before leaving.

Honestly and plainly, John and I never spoke much across the years. Some could argue that even writing this book, I simply spoke to Sue who amplified my questions to a volume that he could hear. It was never a conscious distance but he was content in his well-set lifestyle and I suffered either shyness or a lack of social skills to keep up conversation.

Despite this, I always remember John's presence in my life, even if only in the background. A kindly, sturdy figure that felt like the trunk of our family tree. He and his house felt like immovable constants. Landmarks in our lives. I remember a scrap of an isolated childhood memory, where myself and Diane's daughter Kayleigh would play in John's lounge room whilst the adults elsewhere talked about boring things like motorways.

The most vivid part of the memory is the cushions. The swirling circle patterns in grassy green and daffodil yellow colours. The cushions were enormous and so made effective building blocks with which me and Kayleigh crafted forts and dens and tunnels around and over the sofas for hours.

When visiting John for this book, I stored some recording equipment in that room and was comforted to see the same cushions still there twenty-something years later. I realised immediately of course they were not enormous spongy walls but actually perfectly regular-sized cushions and yet some early memories emblazon themselves upon our minds so strongly like that.

For whatever reason, that is one of mine but it feels indicative of the rich yet cosy atmosphere my memories associate with the place. Grandad's house was always a place of warmth and fun which I believe could have only stemmed from the man himself.

John's family and friends continued to visit him over the following days with Sue and Diane both looking after him every day. My next visit was the afternoon of Saturday 8th with Sue and we arrived to find him stubbornly chewing a ham sandwich with his two remaining teeth. I felt he seemed to be more vibrant and talkative than on Tuesday but Sue and Diane were noticing a more gradual deterioration.

A persistent cough was aggravating him, alongside the necessary but disruptive nurse's checks which left him with very fragmented sleep. He could move a little more but was still ultimately bedridden and required a shifting mattress to avoid bedsores. He claimed the nurses were very good to him at the hospital but there was an evident weariness and irritability in his overall situation.

We took this opportunity to run the title of the book by him as it neared completion. Everyone we'd asked had unanimously favoured "Man Of The Land" but I was keen to have approval from the eponymous man himself. I did my best to speak loudly and clearly but to no avail. After Sue repeated the title back to him he was silent for a few seconds as he mulled it over. "Yeah...Yeah, that's alright. That's fine."

Of the four patients in the ward, typically John's TV was the only one not working so we inquired about bringing him a small radio next time and some earphones to listen to sports broadcasts. I offered up the many spare wired earphones I always carry in my bag in a slightly desperate effort to have some way of helping. We also promised to bring an excerpt of the book to read to him on our next visit.

John passed in his sleep that night, in the early hours of an Easter Sunday morning. The 9th of April 2023, at the age of ninety two. It's unfortunately unclear if John grasped the finality of his situation whilst in hospital. He talked of an eagerness to return home, to his chickens and to his flowers and vegetables. He wondered how long he would be in hospital for.

The terminal nature of things was explained to him but no one could bear to state it too bluntly. Not while it was entirely unknown how long he had left in the hospital's care. On the other hand, he spoke with Sue and Diane about collecting up the many belongings at Parsonage Downs and where to find certain things he would not be returning to, so perhaps there was an awareness and John simply preferred keeping conversations light for everyone else's sake. Incidentally one of these possessions was a grand secret stash of Guinness that John had stocked up on during the pandemic for fear of suddenly not being able to find any.

In some ways, perhaps it is a mercy that his time in hospital was not overly drawn out as he could never truly be comfortable anywhere but home. At the same time, I feel a sorrow for those who didn't have a chance to visit him. I will always regret that he will never be able to read this book despite us knowing this was a possibility from the offset of the project.

Ultimately I try to focus on the wisdom my father gave me as I broke the news to him later that day.

"He doesn't need to read it, he lived it. **It is him.**"

A perspective I hadn't considered but feels intensely poignant and reassuring. In many ways John wrote this book alongside me and I hope it grants a sense of him persisting beyond himself in this form.

John's life wasn't immediately apparent as complex or glamorous but to be so consistently caring, providing, approachable and good jovial company for a near-century of life is a far subtler and far rarer achievement that speaks to a man of vast and enduring moral character. This was recognised, not just by those close to him but by scores of people he met, helped and worked with. And it was great scores of people who turned up to his funeral on Friday April 28th 2023.

That restless morning as the taxi took us to the church, I watched as all the important places in John's life swiped past the window. From Dunmow Town centre with all the shops John would herd cattle past in his youth, every Tuesday morning on market day. Where he found Yvonne and her friend Jean sheltering from the rain and took the chance of asking them out to the Kinema.

His home for close to seventy years, 31 Parsonage Downs. The cosy cottage brimming with memories that became as much a part of John's character as the man himself. Where Yvonne had asked the procession specifically to drive past rather than using the bypass and where Sue and Diane had decorated his gate entrance with branches of a blossoming shrub from his garden.

Then onto Park Road and past the house where he was born. Followed closely by the dirt road turn off adorned with a simple sign marking "Raven's Farm". The cottage of John's childhood just visible in the distance.

Easton Manor and the church rectory grounds where John helped revive the Countess Of Warwick show and won his countless horticultural awards and finally Little Easton Church itself where John sang in the choir as a child, where his daughters would get married, receive church blessings and his grandchildren christened. This was where he was finally laid to rest alongside Alfred, Ethel and Geoffrey nearby.

The small church had almost every seat filled with what was estimated to be close to one hundred attendees all wishing to pay their respects. I recall Sue saying "I had no idea he was such a legend. To me, he was always just Dad." The large crowd made the ceremony initially more daunting for his daughters who stood before them all and gave their tributes to John. Sue gave an insightful and touching retelling of her pivotal memories with her father while Diane read a heartfelt original poem in his honour.

In between these tributes, hymns were sung and prayers made. "Smile" by Nat King Cole was played during the opening and to close "Fields Of Gold" by Eva Cassidy. Myself, my brother (also helpfully called John) alongside other grandchildren and friends decided to be pallbearers for leading John's coffin from the hearse into the church. My being the tallest there made it an awkward and uneven procession but I tried my best to crouch walk with solemn dignity.

As the service ended and we followed the hearse to the plot of land for John's burial, Sue asked me to grab a last minute picture of another tribute set up outside the church. The haphazard photo that follows shows John's scales which Peter found when taking custody of the chickens, cleaned up and had presented by the doors to the church.

These were used for weighing John's many prize-winning pumpkins and upon them rests a red washing basket full of vegetables. I'm told even the washing basket belonged to Yvonne and is a long-standing memory for Sue as a child. Alongside this a pitchfork and atop the scales a can of Guinness, John's drink of choice.

At the gravesite some final words were spoken by Reverend Jo Wood who lead the service and the coffin was lowered into the ground. Yvonne approached the edge and threw two red roses in, followed by Sue throwing a tomato and a ragged old dog toy for the many canine visitors and residents at Parsonage Downs. A basket was brought forward and the rest of the family gently tossed potatoes, runner beans, onions, carrots and other vegetables into the grave.

In some other theatrical context the pelting of vegetables would be seen as a form of disrespect but here it couldn't have been a more polar opposite. We joked about the idea of these offerings taking root around John's coffin and a massive growth of crops rising out from the ground above it. Nothing would be more fitting.

I don't know what type of vegetable I picked up when I stood by the grave and being the sleep-deprived clown I am, I nearly fell in myself. But I thought some final words to John as I threw the plants in and they were promising to do him justice with this book. I hope that I have.

From the coincidental passing of a massive John Deere combine harvester driving by and around the church ahead of the hearse, to Sue's son John wearing his grandfather's shoes after a luggage-restricted flight from Spain. There were signs of John Perry all around us that day. Even when the heavens opened upon arrival to the church, the rain was light and later on the skies cleared into a bright and warm afternoon. As if we got a medley of the seasons to soundtrack the man's life who was so in tune with them.

John spent his life cultivating the land on which he found himself, even as that land and the culture upon it changed around him. He cultivated a family, tended to them and nurtured their growth as a loving and dutiful husband, father, grandfather and great grandfather. He cultivated a legacy of turning nothing but dirt and soil into the bountiful and the beautiful. Nourishing the lives of all those around him. He got the best out of the land and we all blossomed for his efforts until finally the land got to take the best back.

ESSEX EDUCATION COMMITTEE.
Great Dunmow Council Mixed School.

REPORT for Summer Term, 1944

Name: John Perry Age: 13.6
Form: S.II No. in Form: 12 Average Age in Form: 13.3

Max.	Examination Score	Position	Subject	Remarks on working during term	Responsible Teacher
100	75		Reading	V.G.	R.H.W.
100	77		Language (Written)	V.G.	R.H.W.
100	100		" (Spoken)	Excellent	R.H.W.
100	100		Spelling	Excellent	R.H.W.
			Literature	V.G.	R.H.W.
100	90		Handwriting	V.G. indeed	R.H.W.
100	70		Arithmetic (Mental)	On term's work should	R.H.W.
100	40		" (Written)	have shown better result	R.H.W.
			Algebra	F.G.	H.G.
			Geometry	G.	H.G.
100	72		Geography	V.G.	R.H.W.
100	65		History	V.G.	H.L.
			Art	Fairly good	H.L.
100	60		Wood Handwork	V.G.	Mr. Frecknel
			~~Needlework~~		
100	65		Gardening	Good	a.s.
100	62		Science	Good on the whole	a.s.
			Physical Training	Much improved	H.L.
			Games	Excellent	B.P.N.
			Music	V.G.	R.H.W.
1200	876	4			

Conduct: V.G. Attendance: Excellent Punctuality:

General Remarks: A splendid worker and well deserves his position in class (Highest boys total)

R.H. Wilcox — Form Master C.A. Newling — Head Master

A report of John's school grades from his last year in education 1944.

John, Alfred, Sue and baby Diane.

For all his work, there aren't many pictures of John aboard the machines. This might be the earliest, estimated to be sometime in the sixties.

Getting Sue and Diane into the family business.

A present for young Diane and an unprepared bed head on John.

John and Sue during a family coastal trip to the Isle Of Wight in 1967.

John and his daughters biking on holiday.

From left to right: John, Geoffrey, Peter, a family friend and Alfred. The event being Judy and Michael's wedding reception in March 1967.

Similar to the reservoir excavation and located not far from it, John and Peter were also partly responsible for digging the rectory ponds of Little Easton church. Jack Webb and Hubert Rolph were amongst the others who assisted them. The brothers are pictured here in the 1960's with Peter on the left and John on the right.

Some sixty years later, the completed ponds are a charming sight and teeming with aquatic life. Sue and me visited to take this photo in July 2023.

Left to right: Mickey and Dusty above, Lucky and Lady below.

John with one of his awards for floral display .

John's award winning pumpkins and vegetable trays, alongside Judy and Geoffrey's floral displays.

Family's 150 years at farm

by **JAN MOLLER**

A DUNMOW family has clocked up 150 years working at the same farm.

And on Saturday John Perry of Parsonage Downs followed in his father's footsteps and received a medal and certificate for working at Ravens Farm in Little Easton for 51 years.

After the presentation at the Essex Show, the 65-year-old said his late father Alfie received a long service medal from the Queen Mother in 1969 for working 53 years at Ravens Farm.

His younger brother, Peter, has already clocked up 45 years at the farm.

Mr Perry remembers ploughing the fields with horses when he was 14 and progressing to motor driven vehicles through his half a century working life.

He and his wife Yvonne have two daughters and five grandchildren.

Now retired as a farmworker, he nevertheless returns to Little Easton three days a week to tend Bob Trembath's farm garden.

A regular entrant and winner at Dunmow and village horticultural shows, Mr Perry says he will now have more time to spend on his entries.

"I seem to be more busy now than when I was working full-time," he said.

One of several instances of John and the Perry family featuring in local newspapers.

Alf and Ethel Perry

A DECKCHAIR snooze in his beloved greenhouse is 76-year-old Alf Perry's favourite pastime — and perhaps this week his dreams turned to his happy marriage, 50 years old yesterday.

Alf and his wife, Ethel, known as Minnie, who is 78, have lived in the Dunmow area all their lives and were married at Little Easton church, four years after their courtship began at a barn dance in the village.

They moved into their new home in Woodview Road, Dunmow on New Year's Day this year — and in the process 200 of Alf's treasured geraniums perished in the frost.

However he has now built up a new collection of plants and vegetables in his greenhouse and enjoys gardening.

Alf was employed for 62 years as an agricultural worker at Little Easton and was presented with a long-service certificate by the Queen Mother in 1969.

Minnie was a children's nursemaid and recalled looking after Uttlesford councillor Rowena Davey as a child.

The couple, who have four children and four grandchildren, held a party at the Dunmow club ⋯terday for family and friends.

Alfred and Ethel in the late seventies.

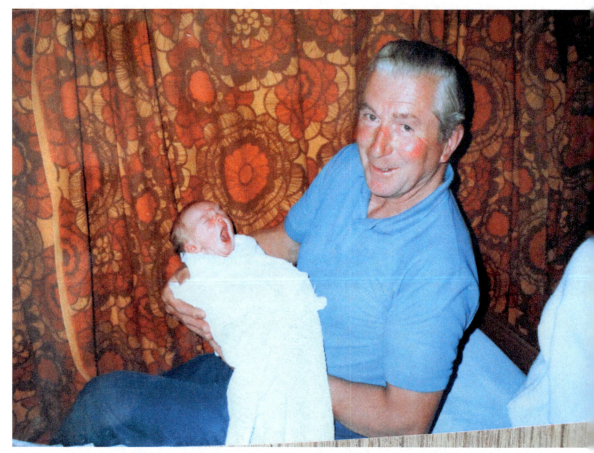
John meets John. His grandson and Sue's first son in 1988.

Everyone's a winner. John with his grandchildren Laura and David sometime in the early 1990's.

John receiving his long service award in 1996 from local businessman Mike Porter.

John and me on a camel ride during a family holiday in Lanzarote, September 2007. We were both gripping the handles extremely tightly but I think John kept his nerves hidden better than me.

Sue and John in his garden at Parsonage Downs in the early 2020's. His chicken run visible in the background.

John once again teaching a new generation of youngsters about gardening. Pictured with his great grandchildren Aleah, Harriet and Arthur in the early 2020's.

John with Sue's dog Alfy in 2022

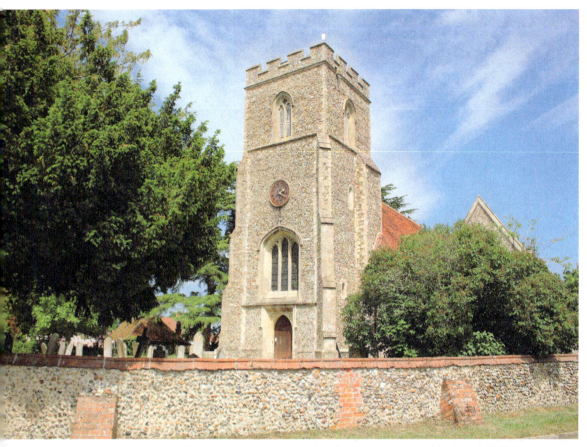

Little Easton church where so many important events in John's life took place. Taken in June 2022.

John and his chickens in 2022